THE
CRYSTAL
ZODIAC

An Hachette UK Company
www.hachette.co.uk

First published in Great Britain in
2021 by Pyramid, an imprint of
Octopus Publishing Group Ltd
Carmelite House
50 Victoria Embankment,
London EC4Y 0DZ
www.octopusbooks.co.uk

This edition published in 2024 by
Godsfield, an imprint of Octopus
Publishing Group Ltd

Distributed in the US by
Hachette Book Group
1290 Avenue of the Americas
4th and 5th Floor
New York, NY 10104

Distributed in Canada by
Canadian Mando Group
664 Annette St
Toronto, Ontario, Canada, M65 2C8

ISBN 978-0-7537-3550-3

A CIP catalogue record for this book
is available from the British Library

Printed and bound in China

10 9 8 7 6 5 4 3 2 1

Publisher: Lucy Pessell
Designer: Isobel Platt
Editor: Feyi Oyesanya
Assistant Editor: Samina Rahman
Production Manager: Allison
Gonsalves
Illustrations: Inna Sinano/
Dreamstime.com; Natali Myasnikova/
Dreamstime.com

THE
CRYSTAL
ZODIAC

ALICE LINDEN

HOW TO USE CRYSTALS TO
READ YOUR FORTUNE

CONTENTS

INTRODUCTION

The Crystal Zodiac is your guide to harnessing the divinatory power of crystals, and is split into several handy sections to help you get started. You will learn how to select and look after your crystals, and will become familiar with the ways in which they can affect your everyday life. You will also learn how to cast crystals onto a zodiac circle, and will find in-depth interpretations of a range of crystals before finally moving onto conducting readings of crystal spreads. At the back of the book, you will find a directory of alternative crystals to use for your zodiac sign, should you need it. As you work through this book, remember to approach crystal divination with an open mind and heart. Work and play with the ideas and methods revealed here, and enjoy discovering what the future holds in store for you.

THE HISTORY OF THE CRYSTAL ZODIAC

As long ago as 4000 BCE the Chaldaean people of Mesopotamia used astrology and the stars to predict the future. They also believed that crystals found in the earth were linked to planets, which reflect the vibrations of the cosmos. From the earliest times crystals have been regarded as possessing divinatory powers: the ancient Greeks believed that every piece of clear quartz crystal is a fragment of the archetypal Crystal of Truth. Each of the 12 signs of the zodiac also corresponds to a crystal, and, in turn, each crystal aligns with the energies associated with that astrological sign.

WHAT CAN CRYSTALS REVEAL ABOUT YOUR FUTURE?

Crystals have been used for fortune-telling throughout history for their subtle vibrational nature, which is thought to be linked to the vibrational powers of the cosmos. They open the gateway to deeper knowledge and your own inner wisdom and intuition. As a divinatory tool, they can be cast onto a zodiac circle to harness the power of the planetary forces and protect against negative energies, or they can be laid out in a spread, like Tarot cards and

runes. Alternatively, you can pick one from a pouch or bag, as your guide crystal for the day. You can also align your own energy to your personal zodiac crystal vibration and benefit from its miraculous properties by wearing the crystal all day long.

THE BENEFITS OF USING CRYSTALS

- Identify influences and energies in your life.
- Learn what challenges you need to overcome.
- Know what sort of day you can expect.
- Discover instant solutions to questions.
- Find your guiding crystal for future happiness.
- Discover what the future holds.

Uncannily, you will find that events and encounters through the day align with the symbolism of that crystal, or that your crystal will empower you with its specific qualities. For example, say you randomly chose aquamarine, the chances are that you will have a flirtatious or romantic encounter!

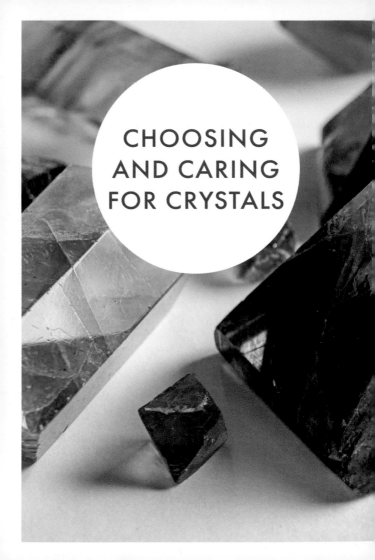

CHOOSING
AND CARING
FOR CRYSTALS

For the crystal zodiac in this book, you ideally need each of the set of 22 crystals overleaf, but if you can't get hold of them all, you can replace some with other crystals associated with the zodiac signs (there are suggested alternatives at the back of the book, or you can ask for help in any New Age shop).

Buy flat, oval-shaped crystals, and hold each crystal in your hand until you 'know intuitively' that it's the one that is right for you. It might feel very cold or very hot, or almost as if it's vibrating in your palm. If you get a reaction – especially an intuitive 'flash' – then you're in tune with the vibrational energy of the crystal and therefore with the cosmos.

Make sure to choose a mixture of active and passive crystals. Active crystals usually work best when you carry them around with you, or if you are placing them on a particular part of your body that needs healing. Passive crystals, on the other hand, can be left on your shelf or bedside table to do their thing.

PASSIVE

 AMBER

 ONYX

 AQUAMARINE

 OPAL

 JADE

 PERIDOT

 LAPIS LAZULI

 ROSE QUARTZ

 MOONSTONE

 TOURMALINE

ACTIVE

 AMETHYST

 OBSIDIAN

 BLUE LACE

 ORANGE

 AGATE

 CARNELIAN

 CITRINE

 RED AGATE

 CLEAR QUARTZ

 RED

 MALACHITE

 CARNELIAN

LOOKING AFTER YOUR CRYSTALS

Once you have chosen your crystals, look after them carefully, as they can sometimes be fragile. To keep them safe, wrap each one separately in a silk scarf. Alternatively, find the right place in your home or office for each crystal, such as on your desk, on your bedside table or as part of an arrangement of houseplants near your favourite chair.

STORING YOUR CRYSTALS

Though harder natural stones can scratch softer ones when they are stored together in a pouch, tumbled stones are in general more resistant to damage. If you don't want to wrap each crystal individually, you can keep a collection of small tumbled stones in a silk bag or pouch.

Crystals that have points are especially prone to damage. Crystals that you want to have on display or that you use frequently can be kept out, but they will need cleansing more frequently because they may pick up what is going on in the room or become polluted by electromagnetic radiation or geopathic stress. Keep crystals out of sunlight, because some stones may fade. However, some exposure to sunlight may be specifically indicated for particular uses, which is a different matter.

CLEANSING YOUR CRYSTALS

All crystals, whether tumbled stones, crystal balls, healing wands or jewellery, should be cleansed before using or wearing because crystals pick up and absorb influences. Some people believe that some crystals never need cleansing (citrine, for instance) but it can never do any harm to cleanse them, even if all that needs removing are the most superficial influences of someone else's touch. Be especially careful of crystals that have been used by another person for esoteric purposes or that have been worn on the body; cleanse these thoroughly before using them.

Crystals are very delicate and should be treated with great care when cleansing. Tumbled stones are tougher because they have been ground to a smooth and durable finish, but they still need respect. Basically, what cleanses your crystal is your intention to do so. If you are good at visualizing, place your crystal in front of you on a white cloth, and simply imagine a stream of pure water flowing through the crystal, deeply cleansing it. Do this visualization for as long as you feel necessary.

If you want to do something more physical, take your crystal to a stream and hold it in the water, while affirming that all impurities are being removed. Or you may soak your crystal overnight in spring water. Never use salt water as it can damage some crystals, and be aware that some crystals, such as selenite, are water-soluble and so should never be cleansed by this method. Crystals should be allowed to dry naturally on a clean cloth; do not rub them.

You can also cleanse crystals by passing them through incense smoke; a lavender joss stick will serve this purpose admirably. Passing them through (or near) a candle flame will also do the trick.

Crystals should be cleansed each time you use them, before being safely stored until next time.

MORE CLEANSING TIPS

- A carnelian kept in a bag with other tumbled stones will keep them all clean.
- Small crystals can be left overnight on a larger crystal cluster of clear quartz or amethyst to be cleansed.

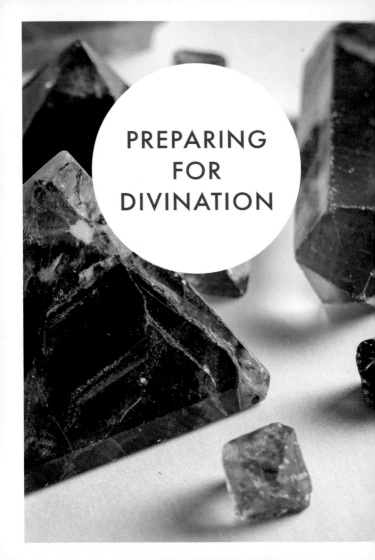

PREPARING
FOR
DIVINATION

After choosing and cleansing your crystals you will want to charge them up with your own essence to make them truly 'yours'. You may do this simply by holding the crystal between your palms and sending energy into it, visualizing the crystal pulsating with the life force that you have imparted.

Alternatively, you may wish to perform a small ritual to charge your crystal and to also dedicate it to divine powers (see overleaf). You will need a candle, a stone, a lavender joss stick and a glass with a stem (such as a wine glass) containing water. If you have a statue of a goddess or god that is meaningful to you, have this close by. You will also need your crystal.

CRYSTAL CIRCLE RITUAL

Affirm that your ritual space is clear. Sweep it with a broom or duster as a symbol of cleansing.

1. Imagine a protective circle surrounding you.

2. Place the stone roughly to your north, the joss stick to the east, the candle to the south and the glass of water to the west. If you live in the southern hemisphere, reverse the positions of the candle and stone. These objects represent the four elements – earth, fire, air and water – and the directions to which they have a time-honoured link in esoteric tradition. Place your statue by the element you prefer.

3. Holding your crystal in your hand, face the stone and say 'I dedicate this crystal to the powers of earth, for grounding and protection'. Move sun-wise (clockwise in the northern hemisphere, anticlockwise in the southern hemisphere) visiting the other elements.

4. Face the joss stick and say 'I dedicate this crystal to the powers of air for clarity and truth'.

5. Face the candle and say 'I dedicate this crystal to the powers of fire for courage and energy'.

6. Face the glass and say 'I dedicate this crystal to the powers of water for healing and purity'.

Now your crystal is truly charged up. Mentally dismantle your protective circle and store your crystal with care.

OPENING YOUR MIND

Before you begin using your crystals for divinatory purposes, you may find it beneficial to practise opening your mind in order to help you more readily accept the power and wisdom of your crystals, and to enhance your intuition during readings. The following exercise is designed to help you do this and asks you to quieten your everyday mind to create space for deeper wisdom and guidance. Before you begin, you will need a sphere of clear quartz, obsidian or smoky quartz and a small white candle.

1. Light the candle and dim the lights in the room. Hold the crystal sphere in your cupped hands for several moments and focus on your breathing, continuing until you feel relaxed and centred.

2. As you hold the sphere, clarify your intention. If you are seeking the answer to a question, state it in words. If you are seeking guidance about a situation, phrase what you wish to know in a clear, positive, open-ended way.

3. Place the sphere in front of you with the burning candle behind it.

4. Gaze at the crystal with half-closed eyes and allow images to form in your mind and on the sphere. Follow any images that appear until you have learned everything that you can.

5. When you feel that the process is complete, acknowledge what you have discovered as the deep wisdom of your own intuition. Wrap the crystal sphere in a cloth and blow out the candle.

YOUR
PLANETARY
CRYSTALS

Each planet in the solar system rules a zodiac sign (apart from Venus and Mercury which rule two signs each) and corresponds to specific energies of the associated crystals. Look up the interpretations over the next few pages when you cast or draw these stones.

Sun	Clear quartz	Active	Clarity
Moon	Opal	Passive	Sensitivity
Mercury	Topaz	Active	Understanding
Venus	Tourmaline	Passive	Compassion
Mars	Red Agate	Active	Progress
Jupiter	Lapiz Lazuli	Passive	Wisdom
Saturn	Onyx	Passive	Structure
Uranus	Orange Carnelian	Active	Rebellion
Neptune	Blue Lace Agate	Active	Vision
Pluto	Amethyst	Active	Passion

THE SUN
RULES LEO

Clear quartz crystal

Like the sun, clear quartz crystal represents direct, potent energy. It is the crystal of action, focus and potential. When you draw clear quartz in a reading you know it's time to act from the heart, to get on with your goals, fulfil those dreams and enjoy being yourself. Wear or carry this crystal if you need to start afresh.

THE MOON
RULES CANCER

Opal

The moon represents intuitive, feeling energy and, similarly, the opal embodies a moody, translucent aura. When you draw your moon crystal in a reading, it reminds you to respect your intuition and your emotions. Wear or carry opal to feel more in tune with others or to develop your sixth sense.

MERCURY RULES
GEMINI AND VIRGO

Topaz

Mercury is known as the planet of 'magical communication', and when you draw topaz it indicates that you must now communicate your desires, open your mind to other ideas and express yourself clearly. Wear or carry your Mercury crystal to aid decision-making or for happy travelling.

VENUS RULES
TAURUS AND LIBRA

Tourmaline

Venus represents beauty, love and affairs
of the heart. When you draw or cast your
Venus crystal, new relationships are favoured
and romance or deeper love will develop.
It's time to use your heart not your head.
Wear or carry tourmaline to promote harmony
and tolerance.

MARS
RULES ARIES

Red agate

Mars is the planet of confidence and desire. And red agate represents this fiery spirit of potent leadership. When you draw or cast red agate, you are ready to defend your rights or those of others. You may feel frustrated by events, but now's the time to initiate what is right for you. Wear or carry red agate when you need a shot of courage.

JUPITER RULES SAGITTARIUS

Lapis lazuli

This stone has always been known as the 'eye of wisdom' and, like Jupiter, represents truth and meaning in life. When you draw lapis lazuli, career matters, wider knowledge and ideals are important to you now. Carry this stone when you want to discover deeper truths.

SATURN RULES CAPRICORN

Onyx

Saturn represents order and definition. When you draw or cast onyx, limitations may be holding you up, but the reality is that your determination will see you through any delays. Realize that it's time to define who you are and your true values. Carry onyx when you want to achieve your goals.

URANUS
RULES AQUARIUS

Orange carnelian

This stone was worn to protect against envy and, like Uranus, it represents freedom from the expectations of others. It's time to make progress and however way-out your thinking, it's through change and rebellion against the status quo that you will become true to yourself. Wear your Uranian crystal when you need to break free.

NEPTUNE
RULES PISCES

Blue lace agate

When you draw your Neptune crystal, it's time to relinquish worn-out ideas and habits and instigate a new vision for your future. Accept that wherever you go you can't escape yourself. Carry blue lace agate if you feel confused and need clarity, or to promote self-awareness.

PLUTO
RULES SCORPIO

Amethyst

Pluto represents our bottom-line survival instinct, our passion for life. Likewise, when worn or carried, amethyst absorbs negativity and allows you to be fearless in the face of change. When you draw the Pluto stone, accept that you have come to the end of one cycle of your life and must now move onto the next with passion and self-belief.

YOUR
ZODIAC
CRYSTALS

The following crystals correspond to each sign of the zodiac and along with the ten planetary crystals, they make up a complete set of 22. Don't worry if you can't get hold of them all. Start with ten that you really like, but make sure there is a good range of colour and meaning.

Ensure that you haven't chosen ten crystals that are all active, with no passive ones. Depending on which sign of the zodiac you are, always carry, wear or keep in a safe place your own zodiac crystal. This will give you confidence, self-belief, vitality and the ability to express your true potential and chosen pathway.

Check the keywords and phrases relating to your sun-sign. If they sound unfamiliar, place the crystal under your pillow to enhance those qualities that you might be lacking in.

ARIES

Crystal: Red carnelian
Keyword: Activate
Active or Passive: Active

Adventure; big-hearted lover; impulsiveness; fiery character; inventive friend; challenges ahead

TAURUS

Crystal: Rose quartz
Keyword: Love
Active or Passive: Passive

Stability; strong-minded lover; material reward; professional opportunity

GEMINI

Crystal: Citrine
Keyword: Communicate
Active or Passive: Active

Need communication to succeed; bubbly lover; fun; adapts to gain rewards

CANCER

Crystal: Moonstone
Keyword: Embrace
Active or Passive: Passive

Domestic issues needing attention; warm, gentle lover; emotions tested; intense feelings

LEO

Crystal: Tiger's eye
Keyword: Inspire
Active or Passive: Active

Dramatic love affair; fiery lover; luck; looking after number one

VIRGO

Crystal: Peridot
Keyword: Discriminate
Active or Passive: Passive

Work opportunities; sensitive lover; going on a diet; order out of chaos

LIBRA

Crystal: Jade
Keyword: Harmonize
Active or Passive: Passive

Romance; seductive lover; harmony; happy
relationship; indecision; rose-coloured glasses

SCORPIO

Crystal: Malachite
Keyword: Transform
Active or Passive: Active

Intense emotions; enigmatic lover; transformation;
changes likely; resolution of money issues; passion

SAGITTARIUS

Crystal: Turquoise
Keyword: Travel
Active or Passive: Active

Optimistic friends; adventurous lover; positive
thinking; imminent travel

CAPRICORN

Crystal: Obsidian
Keyword: Materialize
Active or Passive: Active

Professional happiness; materialistic lover; job promotion; achievement of your best now

AQUARIUS

Crystal: Amber
Keyword: Rationalize
Active or Passive: Passive

Open-mindedness needed to succeed; new ideas; rebellious lover; following your ideals

PISCES

Crystal: Aquamarine
Keyword: Romance
Active or Passive: Passive

Imagination brings rewards; dreamy lover; romance; inability to escape yourself

CHOOSE A
CRYSTAL FOR
A DAY

You can choose a single crystal to find out what sort of day you are going to have.

1. Gently shake your crystals in their pouch or bag and then take one crystal out and place it in the centre of a cloth.

2. Study it, feel what it means to you and look up its interpretation on pages 58–79.

3. Next, take the crystal in your hands, close your eyes and attune yourself to the crystal vibrations. Let its energy flow through your hands and throughout your body; invite the good qualities of the crystal into your world to empower you.

4. Return the crystal to the bag, or keep it in your pocket or a safe place throughout the day to energize you with its specific qualities. Depending on the meaning of the crystal in question, you will know what kind of day you can expect and how to enact and express the energy in a positive, life-enhancing way.

For example, if you chose red agate, you would need to express your feelings honestly or vividly. If you chose jade, you would need to be open to new opportunities and perhaps chance meetings with strangers.

CASTING
CRYSTALS
ONTO
A ZODIAC
CIRCLE

This divinatory method is fun to do. You can either copy the zodiac circle below onto a large piece of paper or cloth, or mark out the circle with thread. Label each section with the zodiac signs.

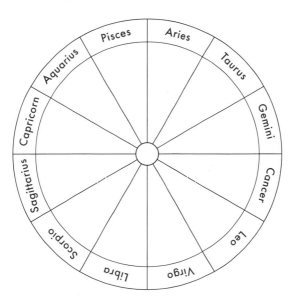

CASTING THE CRYSTALS

Once you have your zodiac circle ready, gather your cleansed crystals and follow the steps below.

1. Place your crystals in a drawstring pouch or bag.

2. Sit or kneel in front of your circle and focus on your particular question. For example, you might want to ask, 'When can I expect new love to come into my life?'

3. Pick a single crystal from the bag, without looking, then cast it onto the circle.

4. Whichever zodiac sign it lands on, check the zodiac keywords on pages 42–45 to help your interpretation.

5. Then draw and cast a second and third crystal.

HOW TO INTERPRET
YOUR CASTING

THE FIRST CRYSTAL

The first crystal you cast is the Crystal of Light. It represents your current situation. It doesn't matter which crystal you throw – it is where it falls in the circle that matters. Say the crystal lands in the slice of the circle devoted to Libra. Turn to the zodiac traits on page 33 to check which qualities Libra signifies. If your question concerned love, this indicates that romance and harmony are favoured right now. The closer the crystal lands to the middle of the circle, the sooner events will unfurl; the nearer the outer edge of the circle, the longer it will take. I usually work on the principle that if it's about halfway between the centre and the edge, this is equivalent to one week; on the edge of the circle is nearer two weeks. If the crystal falls outside the circle, then the time is not yet right for the necessary change or request to take place.

THE SECOND CRYSTAL

The second crystal you cast is the Crystal of Shadows. This represents the people, or outside influences and blockages, which could affect your desires and dreams and which you have to deal with right now. Say the crystal lands on Leo. This indicates that a fiery, progressive friend will be the key to your romantic encounter, but this could indicate a rival – so watch out!

THE THIRD CRYSTAL

The last crystal you throw is the Crystal of Fortune. This indicates the outcome of your question. Say the crystal lands on Gemini, near the edge of the circle. This means that good communication and a light-hearted approach to life will create the romantic dream you're looking for, but you might have to wait for a couple more weeks.

INTERPRETING
CRYSTAL
ORACLES

On the following pages are some simple but varied interpretations of the 22 crystals used throughout this book, from how Citrine can encourage a new start or inspire you to express your creativity, while Aquamarine can help to calm and soothe in moments of vulnerability.

Always widen your interpretation to relate to the question or issue at stake; develop your intuition and work with the vibrational energy of the crystal to help you reach a more detailed analysis.

RED CARNELIAN

Activate, Lead

This is a stone that gives you strength and courage and protects you from negativity and harmful influences from the past.

You may be feeling both excited about what lies ahead but anxious that there may be obstacles in your way. You are driven to succeed. It's time to conquer your fears or self-doubt about what you can achieve.

- Start making headway with your plans now or develop your leadership abilities.

- Someone is pushing their luck or assumes they know what's best for you.

- There will be challenges ahead, but they will bring out the best in you.

ROSE QUARTZ

Love, Sensuality

This stone can help if you have been hurt in the past and need to be able to trust again. It will release repressed emotions and ready you to love and accept the love shown to you by others.

Rose quartz will teach you to and protect yourself by seeking loving and caring company.

- A love match is well-favoured or a great rapport will develop between you and someone new. You are about to fall in love – just make sure that it's not an illusion.

- Sensual pleasure is more important to you than ambition and it's timely to take a break or relax with friends.

- All aspects of relationships can be sorted out now.

CITRINE

Communicate, Transform

Citrine is a stone that encourages making a new start. You can reinvent yourself and your life. Focus on your goals and you will fulfil your ambitions.

Citrine enables you to transform any negative thoughts into positive action. You can make a good decision now, based on logic and objectivity. It is a stone of bright ideas and fun and allows you to express your individuality and creativity.

- Travel is favoured and can bring you happiness.

- Communicate with someone to whom you've never spoken to before and you will learn something valuable.

MOONSTONE

Embrace, Trust

Moonstone helps you get to know yourself at a deeper level. Perhaps you feel distanced from yourself and have lost contact with your inner voice. Trust that there is opportunity to reconnect.

- Trust in your intuition and connect to your inner wisdom.

- Your moods and feelings may be confused, so try to take a more objective look at the issue involved.

- Take care that you aren't being deceived by those who want to have some power over you. Honour your values.

TIGER'S EYE

Inspire, Believe

This is a stone for energy, courage and luck. Tiger's eye will give you the power to identify what you truly need.

Now is the time to dare to be different, and show that you have purpose and vision. Love relationships will be dramatic and challenging.

- You are ready to go on a quest or to inspire others with your talents. Develop your potential and don't let others tell you what you should or shouldn't do with your life.

- Be ambitious and confident but keep in mind to take care of yourself and not overreach.

PERIDOT

Discriminate, Listen

Peridot will show you that it's time to spread your wings, or interact with people who can respect your individuality and not undermine you. You need meaningful relationships, not superficial friends, so choose your company with care. Make decisions based on facts, not on feelings.

- Analyse and keep asking yourself questions. Be sure you are listening to your inner self.

- Discriminate with care, because you will have to make a very important choice in the future.

- Someone is trying to manipulate you – don't let them.

JADE

Harmonize, Assess

Jade is a protective stone and encourages good judgement and awareness of when you might be being coerced or manipulated.

Jade attracts friends who will be positive and supportive influences in your life, so welcome new people in.

- Love and harmony are well indicated, and you will have success in romance. However, don't get wrapped up in sentimentality or become a victim of emotional blackmail.

- You're in harmony with the universe, so ask for what you truly want.

MALACHITE

Transform, Release

Known as the 'sleep stone' because of its apparently hypnotic effect, Malachite indicates that you can transform your life as long as you stay awake to opportunity.

This stone helps you to release negativity and cleanse yourself of negative energies and emotions. This may manifest as the ending of old friendships or relationships that are no longer as close as they once were.

- You're, at last, sailing out of choppy emotional waters into calmer ones. If the issue concerns money or material affairs, you will soon have much success.

TURQUOISE

Travel, Laugh

Turquoise soothes and confers serenity. It gives you space to reflect on simple pleasures and will encourage you to find things that bring you joy and laughter.

- Expand your repertoire of talents and qualities.

- Journeys are indicated, both physical and intellectual ones.

- Watch out for someone who promises the world and can't follow through. Love is boundless.

- Explore your motives: are they your own, or has someone forced you to act the way you do?

OBSIDIAN

Materialize, Persevere

Obsidian is a powerful stone which will reveal long-buried truths or memories that need to be confronted before you progress spiritually.

The stone can help you to transform and offers strength and protection.

- Persevere in your ambitions; don't give in to criticism or self-doubt. There will be challenging influences or setbacks to a plan, but these will in turn instigate a wonderful run of events.

- Welcome any changes, for they will ultimately bring positive results. You can now pursue a goal or aim, and prove your worth.

AMBER

Rationalize, Resolve

Amber encourages creativity, optimism and faith, and clears the mind so that you can work constructively to achieve your ambitions.

Work with amber to dispel feelings of anxiety, stress and depression that may be clouding your vision.

- You are rebellious and visionary, and the time is right to make those radical changes that you know are inevitable.

- Rationalizing a situation, rather than dwelling on the rights and wrongs involved, will resolve the issue.

AQUAMARINE

Hope, Perspective

Aquamarine calms and soothes when you are at your most vulnerable and can bring things into perspective.

Be confident in yourself and don't be afraid to take difficult decisions. Trust that you can cope with any consequences.

- Harmonious feelings and romance are in the air. The tide is turning in your favour.

- Don't let other people's negative emotions get you down, and don't compromise for the sake of peace.

CLEAR QUARTZ

Clarity, Focus

Clear quartz holds the key to knowledge and wisdom. You seek the truth and want the answer to fundamental questions.

Quartz boosts your energy, sharpens your mind and makes you alert yet calm, so tackle problems as they surface.

This stone will bring balance to your life when you need to focus and be free of distractions.

- You can see clearly the way forward out of any difficult situation.

- You will soon be filled with enthusiasm, joy and a sense of personal success. Happiness is within sight, if you believe in yourself.

OPAL

Sensitivity, Release

Opal is an emotional stone and can intensify reactions and experiences.

This stone will help you see that you can't change things that cannot be changed. Accept that someone cannot be anything other than who they are.

- Feelings are running high. Be sensitive to your long-term goals and nurture them.

- Allow feelings of hurt and anger to surface, and be released.

- You are courageous and strong and can be of great spiritual help to close friends, so look around you to see who may need your light.

TOPAZ

Understanding, Consideration

Topaz teaches you that you need to be more open and less judgemental in your relationships. Understanding and tolerance will bring you the results you're aiming for.

If you have an ambition or goal that is not quite fully formed in your mind, now is the time to think about it again, as topaz will help make the next steps clear.

- Someone is making you feel invisible – don't let them.

- Think carefully about a problem, as you will see details you missed before and gain new insights.

TOURMALINE

Compassion, Expression

Tourmaline balances fear with courage, doubt with hope. It is a stone of reconciliation, and encourages you to have compassion and remain level-headed.

- A friend needs you to listen to them without offering advice or passing judgement.

- You will find true love if you respect your own needs. A lover is now ready to commit.

- Tourmaline can also indicate that you've held back on expressing yourself over an issue that has been bothering you and standing in the way of your goals. Speak up for yourself.

RED AGATE

Progress, Power

Red agate is known as 'the warrior's stone' and brings power, decision and determination.
Don't be afraid to persist. Feel emboldened and empowered, and trust you are protected with the gift of emotional endurance.

- You are justifiably angry and it's time to express your feelings – don't bottle them up.

- Progress will be made if you take courage and crusade for your rights.

- A stranger brings unexpected welcome rewards.

LAPIS LAZULI

Wisdom, Equality

Lapis lazuli ensures dignity, equality and clear and honest communication. It also helps the psychic powers, enabling you to tune in to the needs and feelings of others.

- Use your head and not your heart.

- Talk to people who have good advice to offer you or who are very experienced. You can now forge ahead with all career matters.

- Someone has undermined you and damaged your sense of self-worth. Make peace with the past and regain self-respect and equality in that relationship.

ONYX

Structure, Nurture

Onyx will show you that you are now in control of your life, so make sure it is what you want it to be. Structure and organization are needed or you will be in chaos.

Don't give in to fleeting passions or sudden whims. Now is the time to regain control and keep your head clear.

- Material wealth matters to someone more than love.

- Trust yourself above all others and do not share secrets.

- Look after your physical, emotional and spiritual health and regain stamina in these areas.

ORANGE CARNELIAN

Rebellion, Change

Orange carnelian bestows vitality and courage in the face of shifts and changes.

Harness carnelian's fiery energy and fighting spirit and be confident in making spontaneous decisions.

- Innovative and creative change will promote positive life choices.

- Others are frustrating you because they don't agree with your viewpoint, but press ahead with your plans.

- A partner or lover won't commit.

- Ensure you are content on an intimate level with a partner or lover.

BLUE LACE AGATE

Vision, Insight

Blue lace agate encourages you to not overthink situations or problems. Instead, open your mind up and imagine a wide blue sky where thoughts simply pass like clouds.

- Worldly success can be yours if you give as much as you take.

- You have an extraordinary imagination, so make use of it.

- Your vision of the future is great – don't sacrifice it on behalf of others.

- Be sure to speak your mind and clearly communicate your thoughts and feelings to others.

AMETHYST

Passion, Optimism

Amethyst can help you connect with another person at a very deep level and you will find yourself 'knowing' what they feel.

See possibility in new situations and don't be swayed by worries that you are deceiving yourself.

- A passionate love affair is indicated.

- It's time to close one door and open another. There will be a powerful shift in consciousness or a lifestyle transformation for the better.

- Extremes of feeling mean that someone (maybe it's you?) can't decide whether to go or stay, love or hate, give in or resist.

INTERPRETING
CRYSTAL
SPREADS

You can use the crystals as spreads, just as one might use Tarot cards, to ask specific questions, to find out whether you are compatible with someone, for example, and which issues you need to resolve in your life for future happiness.

I have offered sample readings for two of the spreads to help you begin, but you'll soon become familiar with the crystals and their properties and possible meanings.

PREPARING FOR THE SPREADS

Ideally, use a special cloth or silk scarf on a table for these readings. Alternatively, the most natural place to read crystals is out in the open: near the sea, on a beach or in a garden. The crystals are particularly powerful around the crescent and full moon cycles and at specific times of the year, such as the spring and summer equinox and the summer and winter solstices.

Always prepare by relaxing. You can try using a meditation technique, burning incense or lighting candles; or, if you are outside, cast an imaginary magical circle around you by pointing with your finger in a huge circle as you turn 360 degrees. First, cast the circle clockwise, then anti-clockwise – this will protect you and your crystals and will vitalize your own energy to resonate with the cosmos.

If you are tense and anxious, or struggling to relax through meditation or other techniques alone, you can work with a relaxation crystal.

1. Find somewhere comfortable to sit or lie down and place all of your crystals next to you.

2. Close your eyes and concentrate on your body. First, focus on your feet, feeling all the muscles in them, tensing slightly and then relaxing. Now move on up your legs, tensing and relaxing, then focus on your pelvis, buttocks, internal muscles, abdomen, back, chest and shoulders. Travel down your arms, into your fingers, clenching your fists and relaxing. Finally, the muscles in your neck, jaw, face and scalp need the screw-up-and-relax routine.

3. Now let your mind wander to a beautiful, calm place. Take in the sights and the sounds and smells. Perhaps there's a gentle breeze on your skin. This is your happy place.

4. Remain there and think about your crystals. You may immediately get a vivid sense of one crystal. If so, go with this choice, or slowly open your eyes to look at them. The crystal you choose is your relaxation crystal.

DESTINY

This simple spread enables you to find out which issues need to be resolved for your future happiness.

Pick a total of five crystals from your pouch, and lay them out in the order shown below:

1. Your current mood
2. Your future desire
3. What you really want
4. The issue that needs resolving
5. Direction/outcome

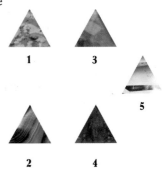

HOW TO INTERPRET THE SPREAD

Each crystal represents a different aspect of your own destiny.

Example reading:

1. Your current mood – **turquoise:**
   You're restless and have itchy feet.

2. Your future desire – **malachite:**
   You're dreaming of material success.

3. What you really want – **amethyst:**
   Deep down you want more passion in your life.

4. The issue that needs resolving – **red carnelian:**
   You need to sort out whether your aspirations are really your own.

5. Direction/outcome – **clear quartz crystal:**
   You will soon have clarity about your true goals.

COMPATIBILITY

This spread is useful when you want to know if someone's energy is compatible with your own. Do you have an affinity with a new friend? Can you trust a rebellious colleague? Is a new lover going to be a perfect match?

Pick five crystals, one crystal at a time, and lay them out in the order shown below.

1. Me now
2. The other now
3. Together now
4. Your test
5. Your destiny together

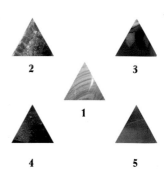

HOW TO INTERPRET THE SPREAD

Each crystal represents a different element of the relationship in question.

Example reading:
Let's say you've recently been promoted at work, but a once-friendly colleague seems to dislike you – can you be friends again?

1. Me now – **blue lace agate:** You feel as if you've sacrificed a friendship for your goals. There are too many undercurrents of feeling and you can't work happily.

2. The other now – **tourmaline:** Your colleague is a compassionate, warm-hearted person, but dares not reveal that she's envious of your success.

3. Together now – **red agate:** If you get together now, the chances are you will have a big row,

expressing all your anger at each other and then get on with work again, but she'll still be seething. It won't necessarily resolve the issue.

4. Your test – **lapis lazuli:** Your test is to widen your social network, make new friends and work contacts and laugh. Be the progressive person you are and place value on those who admire you for your skills.

5. Your destiny together – **amber:** She will soon be objective enough to realize that her behaviour is childish and you will become friends again.

WHAT'S GOING ON TODAY?

This spread is a simple way to get to know the crystals on a daily basis. Apart from just drawing one daily crystal to give you a flavour of the day's events, this easy layout requires little effort and allows you direct experience of the crystals' meanings with a little self-questioning.

Pick three crystals, one crystal at a time, and lay them out in the order shown below.

1. What is the important event of the day?
2. What needs attention/action?
3. What do I need to watch out for?

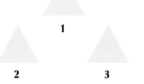

MY PRIORITIES

In daily readings you can also work out what needs attention right now. Sometimes we focus our attention on work rather than relationships and vice versa. This simple spread will get you thinking about what needs to be done first and what things may get in the way of you achieving that particular object or goal for the day.

Pick five crystals, and lay them out in the order shown.

1. What is my priority right now?
2. What is stopping me?
3. What things can I change?
4. What things must I accept?
5. Outcome?

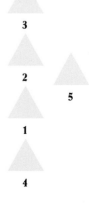

WHAT DO I NEED?

This is a simple yet revealing spread when you're not sure what you need in life or where you're going. Be honest with yourself and remember your needs and wants change with time, so you can do this spread quite regularly.

Pick five crystals, one crystal at a time, and lay them out in the order shown.

1. Who am I now?
2. What/who do I need?
3. What/who don't I need?
4. Options available?
5. Future direction?

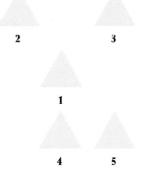

HOW TO SORT IT OUT

We all encounter difficulties in our relationships, and often wonder 'what next, where do we go from here, how can we deal with it?' This spread tells you what the key to the problem is, what to do about it and the future potential.

Pick six crystals, and lay them out in the order shown below.

1. What is the situation now?
2. What is causing the problem?
3. What have we forgotten to respect?
4. What do we need to express?
5. Options available?
6. The future potential?

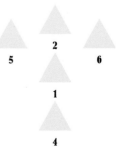

MY SECRETS

This spread is self-revelatory. It tells you what you really want, but you must be prepared to be totally honest when you interpret this layout. It's only our fear of accepting our inner desires that prevent us from moving on.

Pick seven crystals, and lay them out in the order shown below.

1. What is my secret love?
2. What is my secret hate?
3. What is my secret desire?
4. What is my secret test?
5. What puts me off?
6. What motivates me?
7. What can I accomplish right now?

1   **3**

2   **4**   **5**   **6**   **7**

ALTERNATIVE CRYSTALS

ARIES
- **Kyanite** | Blue-Grey | Mental Clarity, Meditation, Decisions
- **Hematite** | Red, Silver | Originality, Inner confidence, Protection

TAURUS
- **Rhodonite** | Pink or Red | Patience, Seeking, Forgiveness
- **Selenite** | White, Orange, Blue, Brown, Green | Connection, Clarity, Manifestation

GEMINI
- **Apophylite** | White, Yellow, Clear, Peach, Green | Release, Attunement, Astral Travel
- **Sapphire** | Blue, Black, Yellow, Pink, Green, Purple | Abundance, Joy, Destiny

CANCER
- **Unakite** | Pinky-Orange, Green | Decisions, Expression, Releasing
- **Ruby** | Red | Passion, Courage, Consciousness

LEO

- **Labradorite** | Grey, Black, Yellow | Psychic Development, Meditation, Responsibility
- **Sunstone** | Orange, Yellow, Red-Brown | Good Fortune, Willpower, Originality

VIRGO

- **Jasper** | Red, Brown, Green, Blue, Purple, Yellow | Unfolding, Nurturing, Manifesting, Continuity
- **Amazonite** | Blue, Green, White | Clarity, Communication, Emotional Balance, Courage

LIBRA

- **Iolite** | Grey, Violet, Yellow, Blue | Grounding, Focus, Intuition
- **Chrysoprase** | Apple-Green, Lemon | Nature, Calming, Accepting, Universal

SCORPIO

- **Smoky Quartz** | Light Brown, Sometimes Yellow or Black Hues | Grounding, Clarity, Calming
- **Rhodocrosite** | Red, Pink, Orange | Calming, Mindful, Revealing

SAGITTARIUS
- **Charoite** | Lavender, Purple | Psychic Power, Transmutation, Intuition
- **Wulfenite** | Golden, Orange, Yellow | Feelings, Cycles, Integrating

CAPRICORN
- **Azurite** | Blue | Balance, Clarity, Focus Spiritual
- **Garnet** | Red, Pink, Green, Orange, Yellow, Brown, Black | Fertility, Abundance, Expansion

AQUARIUS
- **Atacamite** | Turquoise, Green, Green-Black | Self-Motivation, Cleansing, Enthusiasm
- **Magnetite** | Black | Meditation, Visualization, Trust

PISCES
- **Fluorite** | Purple, Green, Brown, Yellow, Blue, Clear | Spiritual Peace, Focus, Connection
- **Smithsonite** | Blue-Green, Pink, Lavender, Purple, Brown, Yellow, White | Soothing, Nurturing, Accepting